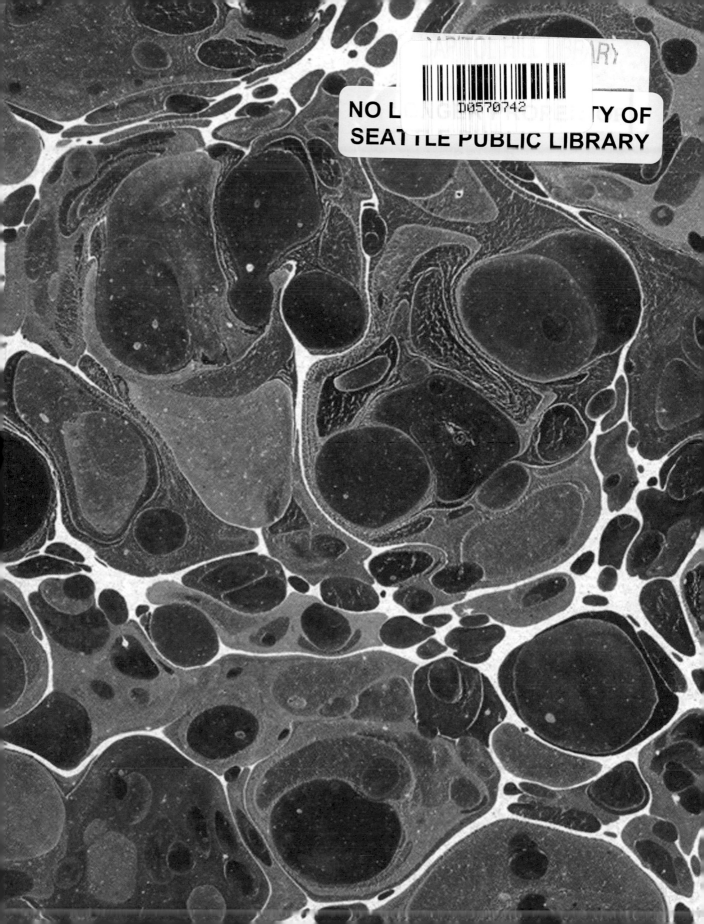

BEHIND CLOSED DOORS.

BEHIND CLOSED DOORS.

THE PRIVATE HOMES OF 25 OF THE WORLD'S MOST CREATIVE PEOPLE

ROB MEYERS

003.

hardie grant books

MELBOURNE · LONDON

DEDICATION.

3 WOMEN

This book is dedicated to the three generations of spectacular homemakers in my life: my mum, who taught me that perfection doesn't make a home; love does. My sister, who taught me that a house isn't a home unless it's filled (to the rafters) with a family. And my magnificent nanna, who taught me at age seven the importance of washing skirting boards and vacuuming the inside of my wardrobe, monthly.

007.

CONTENTS.

PREFACE 013

FOREWORD BY 031
RUPERT THOMAS

INTRODUCTION 037

COURTNEY LOVE 039

LORD PEREGRINE 051
+ CATHERINE ST
GERMANS

JEREMY SCOTT 065

AIMEE MULLINS 077

CHRISTOPHER 081
SIMMONDS

MARTHA STEWART 089

MR + MRS LORIMER 099

MATTHEW STONE 111

TERENCE KOH 121

OLIVIER THEYSKENS 131

VINCE ALETTI 141

KYLE STEWART 153
+ JO SINDLE

CONTENTS.

163   MARVIN SCOTT JARRETT

173   GARY CARD

183   OLEG DOU

191   MARC QUINN

201   CONOR DONLON

211   TAVI GEVINSON

221   SIMON FOXTON

231   MARTIN RAYMOND + CHRIS SANDERSON

239   NICOLA FORMICHETTI

253   THANK YOU

255   ABOUT THE AUTHOR

009.

PREFACE.

HOW IT ALL BEGAN

This book began in 2007, when a friend told me how amazing a mutual friend's house was. I visited and fell in love with their interior style; it was so personal, strong, vibrant, intimate and for the most part, unseen. I left feeling inspired, but also a little sad that I didn't get to live there. Over the next few days I couldn't stop thinking about this space.

I've always been fascinated by interiors. My mum worked in interior design in the late 80s and early 90s and memories of that time have stuck; whether the beauty of bold and innovative modern spaces or the hell of hand-ragged walls and chintz on chintz that persisted as a hangover from the 1980s.

By the time I visited the aforementioned home of note, I was interning between fashion and style bibles *POP* and *Arena Homme+*, and working with some big personalities, big looks and even bigger egos — it was and is all part of the fun. And I started to wonder what all these incredible characters' homes looked like. What if someone who was perfectly polished and put together in public actually lived in a hoarders' dream-home? Would their perfectly pressed camel coat really have been pulled from a poky wardrobe, the moth holes hidden on the inside? Perhaps. Perhaps not. But I was intrigued. So I started asking people to share their homes.

Using my own home as a starting point, I shot a single roll of film and sent the results, along with a letter asking for the same, to the first few contributors — after all, why would people share their homes if I wouldn't share mine, I reasoned? Then, to my surprise, people started saying yes. They seemed to like the idea that it was non-intrusive. I wasn't going to visit myself and they could choose what to share.

Then the cameras started coming back — and they're still coming. Some of the photos surprise me, some don't. But they all inspire me. Sometimes I get a whole house, other times it's just one room. Sometimes I get the full twenty-seven images back, sometimes my contributors only choose to take ten images. And

013.

sometimes, just occasionally, I get one image – but sometimes one image is all you need.

I think the most amazing thing about this process is that, for the most part, the homeowners themselves don't see the images before I do. They shoot blind and return the camera undeveloped, generous and trusting, not knowing what it contains. So I hope they're as excited to see these images now as I am when I first receive a camera back in the mail and rush to have it developed.

A lot of people ask: why a disposable camera? Why don't you just go to the house yourself and shoot it 'properly'? And my response is always the same: if I was coming over to your house, and I'd never seen it before, would you make the bed and tidy up and artfully arrange things before I arrive? Most people say 'yes, of course', and then they realise the purpose of the project. It's not about capturing a 'perfect home', it's about revealing a personal space; taking those quiet moments and sharing them with myself and a wider audience.

This project has been running now for five years. It began life as part of my final year project at Central Saint Martins and was then developed by London-based Garage magazine, who helped me source some amazing homes after inviting the 'Behind Closed Doors' concept into the pages of their biannual art and fashion publication. Then, I continued it on my own, sometimes leaving it untouched for months, other times working on it frenziedly as cameras flowed in from across the world on a daily basis. Finally, it's ready to share.

The following pages showcase twenty-five homes – personal favourites selected by me and my small team. Thank you to those that have had the generosity and kindness to take a simple disposable camera and walk around their private space pressing a simple plastic button twenty-seven times. I hope you enjoy it.

019.

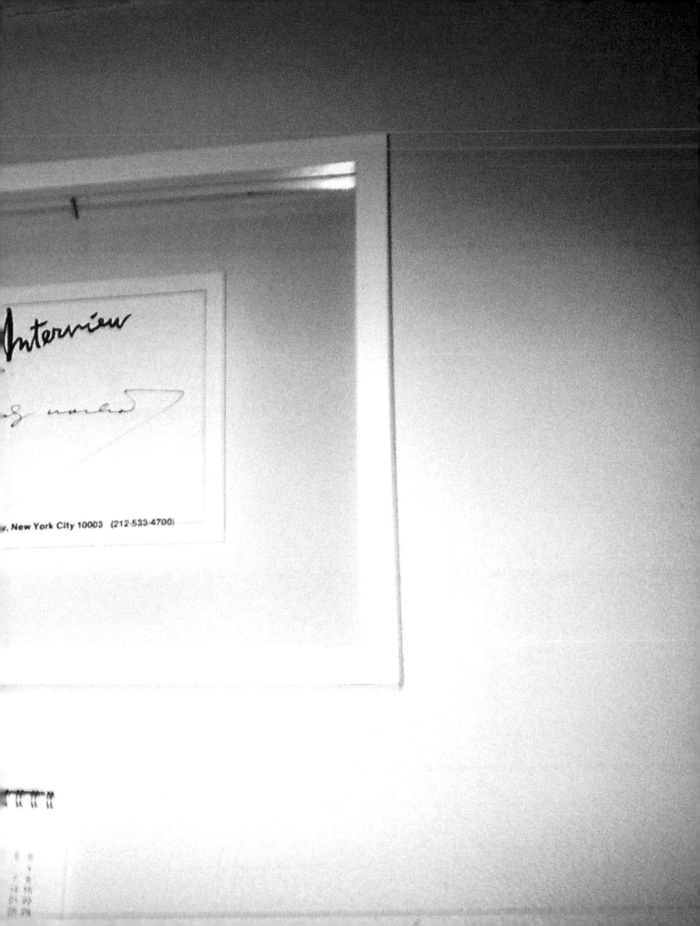

Interview

Andy Warhol (signature)

, New York City 10003   (212-533-4700)

023.

FOREWORD.

'BEHIND CLOSED DOORS AS A CONCEPT'

ow would you react if someone asked you to photograph where you live? Exactly what you shoot will be up to you. And here's a ready-loaded Happy Snap camera just to make the experience even more effortless. Just point and press.

You'd imagine such open-ended flattery would be hard to resist? But my guess is that it's never quite as easy as that. Having undertaken related projects myself, I can vouch for the fact that a keen 'I'd love to' can often turn to a lukewarm 'I'm sorry, there just wasn't time', just as the deadline looms. So I have nothing but admiration for Rob Myers who has pulled off this project with aplomb. Such contributor-led productions can be an agony and an ecstasy. But they can also be well worth the hassle.

Obviously every house is a portrait of its owner. The things they — we — leave out are as telling as the things they leave in. But whereas in conventional magazine we glimpse interiors through the prism of that title's house style, in *Behind*

031.

dwellings? The book positively pulsates with phalluses both photographic and painted. I've clearly been missing a trick.

Rob Meyers' clever and well thought out decision to give contributors control over how we see where they live has paid dividends. This is a book that does what its cover promises: allows a scintillatingly voyeuristic glimpse behind the public facade of some clever, creative and refreshingly individual people.

Rupert Thomas
Editor
The World of Interiors

Closed Doors the contributors have been left to their own devices. So here are unexpurgated self portraits taken by stars from music and fashion, incumbents of a wonderfully crumbling country house and owners of idiosyncratic urban apartments. Of course the things these people have chosen to show are as keenly edited as artful magazine shoots which feature armfuls of flowers and cushions plumped to within an inch of their lives. The seemingly spontaneous rumpled beds and messy shelves are just as orchestrated. And, to me at least, all the more telling and interesting they are for that.

The things shared are as varied as you'd hope, from the expected piles of magazines and books, to a surprising collection of wedding-cake figurines. And who knew so many male genitals would be dangling around these

032

035.

INTRODUCTION.

WELCOME

Welcome. Welcome to my home – and twenty-five other awe-inspiring, jealousy-inducing and genuinely personal homes – and welcome to a project that has been quietly bubbling away in the background of my life for the last five years. It's only now that this first edition feels ready to share on a larger platform than the little blue folder which it was sitting in on my desktop.

In a world of websites, blogs, tumblrs, and every other type of image-hauling platform you can think of / post on / repost from / tweet about / retweet about / like and basically become totally numb to, we seem to have forgotten the simple things. That moment when you turn your phone, iPad, or computer off (the idea scares me too), and just look at what's actually around you. Your world. Your space. Your nesting spot. Whether it's somewhere you have lived for years, or only a matter of months, your home is your sanctuary. You may live in one room, or you may be lucky enough (like some of the homeowners), to have a plethora to choose from. You may be a student, an investment banker, a fashion designer or a stay-at-home mum. It makes no difference – a home is a home. Your space is your space.

And here I would like to share twenty-five very personal spaces, photographed by the owners themselves, on simple disposable cameras. From rock stars and artists to entrepreneurs and journalists, they've laid bare their intimate spaces, capturing what makes each home special and unique. It may be a favourite piece of furniture or the light in a certain room at a particular time of day – whatever makes it theirs.

I hope you enjoy poring over the pages of this book as much as my subjects loved taking the images – and I loved going behind their closed doors.

Rob Meyers
Editor and curator of *Behind Closed Doors*

037.

COURTNEY LOVE.

NEW YORK, USA

 Courtney Love needs little introduction: legendary Hole frontwoman, critically acclaimed musician, grunge style-icon, reformed wild-child. As *Rolling Stone* put it, she is simply 'the most controversial woman in the history of rock'.

Her home is not what a lot of people would expect. It's filled to the brim with stunning, carefully restored antiques set amid soft colour palettes and glowing low lights. The walls are covered; with everything from Damien Hirst pieces to antique lace dresses and ballet pointe shoes. I love the intimate memoirs that Courtney has amassed; her collection of wedding cake toppers and the wall of press clippings covering the doors of her walk-in wardrobe, for instance. But perhaps most notable are the personal photographs that Courtney has chosen to share, including a dinner shot of her, Donatella Versace and Elizabeth Taylor, and most wonderfully, a photo of her late husband Kurt Cobain playing with their daughter, Frances Bean.

039.

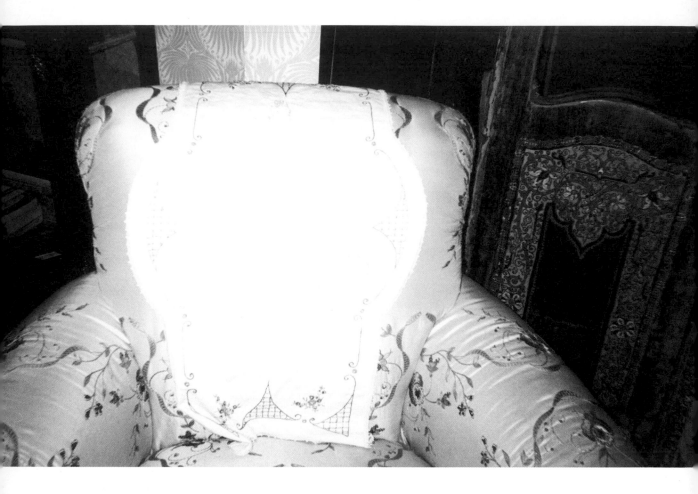

043.

048

LORD PEREGRINE + LADY CATHERINE ST GERMANS.

CORNWALL, ENGLAND

Peregrine Eliot has lived in Port Eliot, his family's estate in Cornwall, since birth. He became head of the household and inherited his title, tenth Earl of St Germans, after the death of his father in 1988. His wife Catherine, a former journalist, has lived in Port Eliot since they married in the orangery, in 2005. Catherine has since turned the estate into a home for the thriving Port Eliot Literary Festival, held every year in the grounds of the house.

The ancient stately house of Port Eliot is a fascinating vision of faded grandeur, and an Aladdin's cave of private family history. The spectacular morning room, which is filled with early boulle furniture, Persian rugs and the most spectacular dark crimson damasks, was last decorated in 1892. The circular drawing room houses Lord Eliot's 1938 Harley-Davidson, on which he travelled across Europe in the 1960s. My favourite piece is a stunning late seventeenth-century Baroque half-tester bed clothed in its original worn, gold-hued fabrics, bought from Christopher Gibbs in the 1960s.

051.

054

055.

056

057.

058

063.

JEREMY SCOTT.

LOS ANGELES, USA

Missouri-born Scott studied in NYC and started his career as a fashion designer in Paris in the mid-90s, under the iron fist of Karl Lagerfeld. By the end of the decade, he'd shown his own ready-to-wear collections across the globe and gained a reputation for striking, pop-inspired clothing. He has designed custom looks for many stars, including Britney Spears' iconic air-hostess uniform worn in her video for 'Toxic', as well as special outfits for Miss Piggy. He is best known for his awe-inspiring collaborations with brands like Longchamp, Swatch and Smart cars and his long-running line of trainers for Adidas. His most recognisable design for the company is the bestselling 'winged' shoe, worn by everyone from Madonna to Björk.

Scott's West Hollywood home was one of the first 'modern' homes shot for this project — and what a home! A classic mid-century modern space, it's filled with spectacular signature pieces, from the marble bust of his own head, to the goat-hair sofa. His collection of self portraits — including one in which he appears as a Roman warrior — sit effortlessly next to his baby grand piano and incredible collection of 1980s postmodern Memphis furniture pieces.

065.

068

072

073.

AIMEE MULLINS.

NEW YORK, USA

Aimee Mullins is a woman who made lemonade when life gave her lemons. Born with a rare medical condition that led to the amputation of both legs when she was only a year old, Aimee went on to compete in the 1996 Atlanta Paralympics and was later appointed Chef de Mission for the USA at the 2012 London Olympics. In 1999 she famously walked in late fashion designer Alexander McQueen's S/S show in a pair of custom-carved prosthetic legs made from solid ash. She has since modelled for brands and publications across the world.

Aimee was one of very few participants who suffered the project's one possible downfall – equipment failure. Her disposable camera jarred after only a few frames, only one of which came out: a shot of her artificial legs elegantly lined up on a monochromatic rug.

They say less is more, and in Aimee's case, this is entirely true.

077.

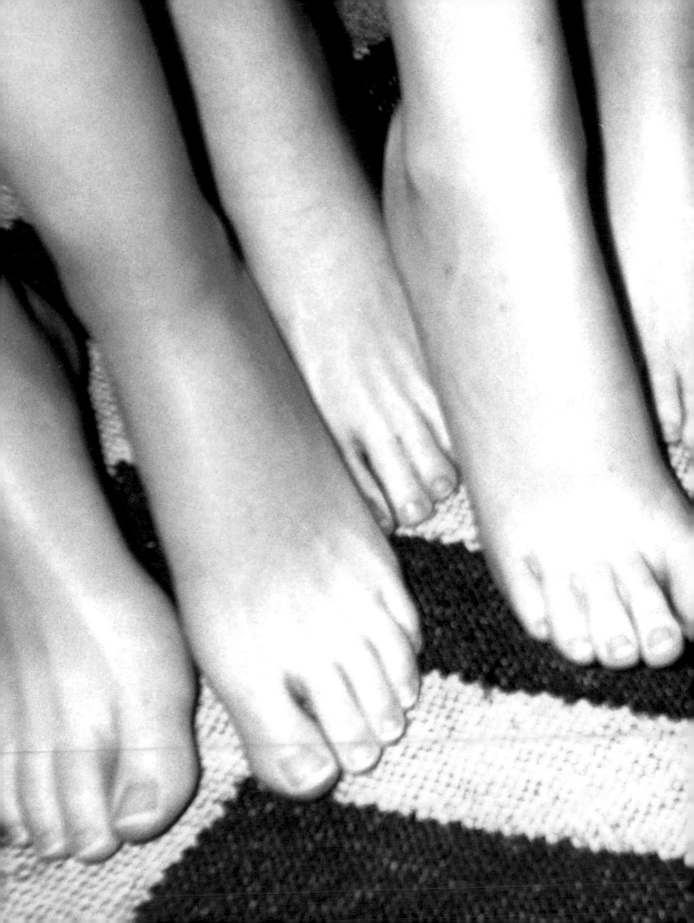

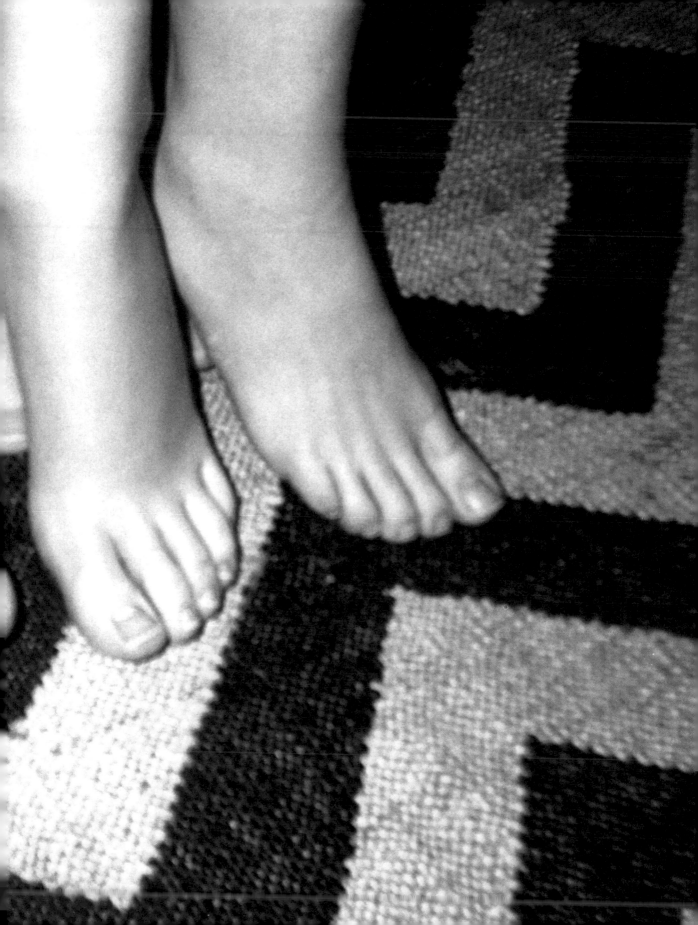

CHRISTOPHER SIMMONDS.

LONDON, ENGLAND

Christopher Simmonds is the Creative Director of London style bible *Dazed and Confused* and the founder of Simmonds ltd., a creative design studio that has worked with the likes of Alexander Wang, Chanel, Stella McCartney and Vivienne Westwood.

Simmonds' personal interior style is linked perfectly in taste and tone to the work he creates for some of the world's biggest fashion houses. Minimal mid-century pieces contrast with mountains of books, visual references and the latest edition to the home, his beautiful three month old Shiba Inu dog, Kenny.

My favourite parts of Simmonds' home feature his work — frame upon frame of beautifully mounted imagery, from Ari Marcopoulos' shots of new-school hip hop prodigy A$AP Rocky for *Dazed and Confused* magazine above the toilet, to iconic Larry Clark prints and Araki polaroids in the lounge, or the archive poster imagery from Vivienne Westwood and Raf Simons scattered throughout the space.

081.

085.

RAF SIMONS SPRING-SUMMER 2003

086

087.

088

MARTHA STEWART.

NEW YORK, USA

 Martha Stewart . . . what can you say? Bastion of the home / cooking / craft / interiors / broadcasting and publishing world, Martha is a lifestyle guru, wildly successful businesswoman, and brand owner.

Martha was one of those people who chose to edit her home very well (would you expect anything less?), shooting only her spectacular kitchen at her farmhouse in Bedford, New York State. When Martha moved into the house she decided she wanted a big kitchen, knocking out six small rooms and hallways from the previous house footprint, leaving her with a magnificent 750 sq ft space to play with. Play she certainly has, filling the open-plan area with a combination of professional steel equipment, homely soft dove-grey wood, elegant flatware, linens and glassware, and of course her French bulldogs, Francesca and Sharkey.

097.

MR + MRS LORIMER.

NORTH YORKSHIRE, ENGLAND

The 'White Lodge' in Harrogate, North Yorkshire, is one of those houses that once viewed, you never forget. Bought by its current owners, Mr and Mrs Lorimer, in 2001, it was the ultimate over-printed, over-pelmetted, over-ruffled hangover from the 1980s, in the shell of a white Modernist spaceship.

The couple spent the next 10 years taking it back to its former Mid-Century Gropius-inspired glory, unveiling its stunning history along the way. Built in 1935 by Newcastle born architect Colonel R.B Armistead, the current owners are the eleventh inhabitants of the home.

The house is striking and elegant, from its polished chestnut entrance hall to the sprawling glass-wrapped formal lounge. It also features handsome fitted sycamore bookcases, juxtaposed angles of graceful Eames and Robin Day furniture, and in the stunning curved dining room, original Betty Joel built-in sideboards. But the most aweinspiring thing of all is the space itself, gushing with light, filled with fresh air, no matter what the season. It's one of those homes that feels like all the hard work in restoring it was well worth it, as residing in such a space on a daily basis would be an absolute joy.

103.

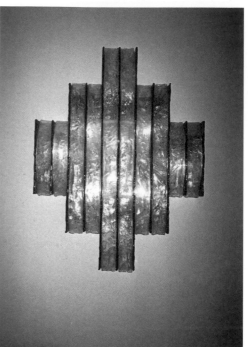

WHITE LODGE

104

105.

108

109.

MATTHEW STONE.

LONDON, ENGLAND

Artist and self-appointed 'shaman' Matthew Stone is a true Renaissance man. From his amazing imagery to his teachings in 'optimism as a cultural rebellion', he effortlessly interweaves his art and cultural provocation with more commercial editorial activity, earning him the number one arts spot in the *Times*' 'Power players Under 30' list.

Matthew's home in east London doubles as his studio and UK crash pad, filled with pieces of his art, religious iconographic references, and memoirs of his !WOWOW! art collective past. My favourite part of his home is an image that perfectly demonstrates the rawness of the 'Behind Closed Doors' idea — a striking monochrome bust portrait hanging on a white brick wall, with a perfectly curated, and I'm sure accidentally-in-shot, can of furniture polish sitting below it.

116

117.

TERENCE KOH.

NEW YORK, USA

Chinese-Canadian artist Terence Koh has been producing largely monochromatic artworks involving queer, punk and pornographic sensibilities since the early 2000s. His luxuriously decadent and sensual pieces have been exhibited around the world. Two years ago, Terence married his long-term partner Garrick Gott, wearing his mother's wedding dress and wrapping himself in 30 ft of white tulle. Last year, he adopted his first child.

Terence's New York home is, as you may expect, white. All of it, everywhere

122

123.

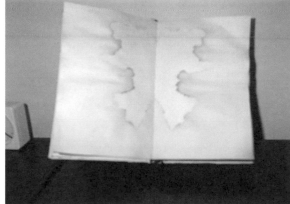

OLIVIER THEYSKENS.

NEW YORK, USA

Belgian-born fashion designer Olivier Theyskens has worked for several major fashion houses including Rochas, Nina Ricci and Theory, where he is now artistic director. Theyskens gained a reputation in the early 2000s for the anti-capitalist purity of his approach to fashion; he refused, for example, to create an accessories line for Rochas in an attempt to 'stop global vulgarity'. He later became the go-to designer for 'demi couture' – using custom haute-couture dressmaking techniques with a more casual retail market in mind – and became a favourite of Madonna, Kirsten Dunst and Nicole Kidman.

Oliver's home also carries traits of high-meets-low culture, from his Lego 'sculpture' of 'Fallingwater' the famous house designed by Frank Lloyd Wright, to his collection of Victorian dolls' eyeballs and mauve- and burnt umber-hued shells cased in a rusting glass cabinet. My favourite feature is his selection of classic Chanel fragrances, nonchalantly scattered along a marble fireplace, flanking a fairly racy illustrative piece.

134

135.

139.

140

VINCE ALETTI.

NEW YORK, USA

Vince Aletti is credited with writing the first ever piece on the American Disco movement for *Rolling Stone* magazine in 1973 and was senior editor at *The Village Voice* for over twenty years. In 1998, he began his curatorial career with an art exhibition in New York, 'Male', followed up in 1999 by 'Female', which both garnerned rave reviews. He is currently a regular reviewer for the *The New Yorker*.

Aletti's home is a credit to his taste and personal art collection, piled high with unnamed photographs of which only he knows the date and origin (every last one!), alongside artworks by Andy Warhol, Nan Goldin, Larry Clark and Alexandr Rodchenko, to name but a few. It is a striking spectacle of a home, and one of my favourites to date.

144

146

147.

151.

KYLE STEWART +
JO SINDLE.

LONDON, ENGLAND

Kyle Stewart and Jo Sindle are the genius minds behind London fashion and lifestyle store Goodhood in Hoxton, London. Opened only five years ago, it has become a fixture on the map of 'East London cool'. Their motto, 'selected goods for the independent mind', truly sums up their ethos — both commercially and privately.

Sindle and Stewart's traditional Victorian two-storey workers' house is nestled in a quiet street, ten minutes' walk from their store, and is a clear footprint of their taste.

This classic building is filled to the brim with modern references ranging from skate to pop culture. Felix the Cat prints hang next to Epcot Centre American registration plates, while Supreme rugs lie across whitewashed oak floors. The home perfectly showcases their style mix of Scandinavian minimalism and American maximalism.

153.

154

156

157.

161.

MARVIN SCOTT JARRETT.

NEW YORK, USA

Marvin Scott Jarrett is responsible for shaping the face of modern youth publishing. He has founded and edited various notable publications, including iconic American music and subculture magazine *RayGun* in the 90s and later, seminal New York youth style bible *Nylon*. His cutting-edge, experimental design and editorial philosophy defined for many the grunge aesthetic of 'Generation X'.

Scott Jarrett's New York home is simple and clean, reflecting a life constantly on the go (see permanently half-unpacked suitcases). It's perhaps more a crash-pad than his homely California space, where he and his wife spend most of their downtime.

163.

166

167.

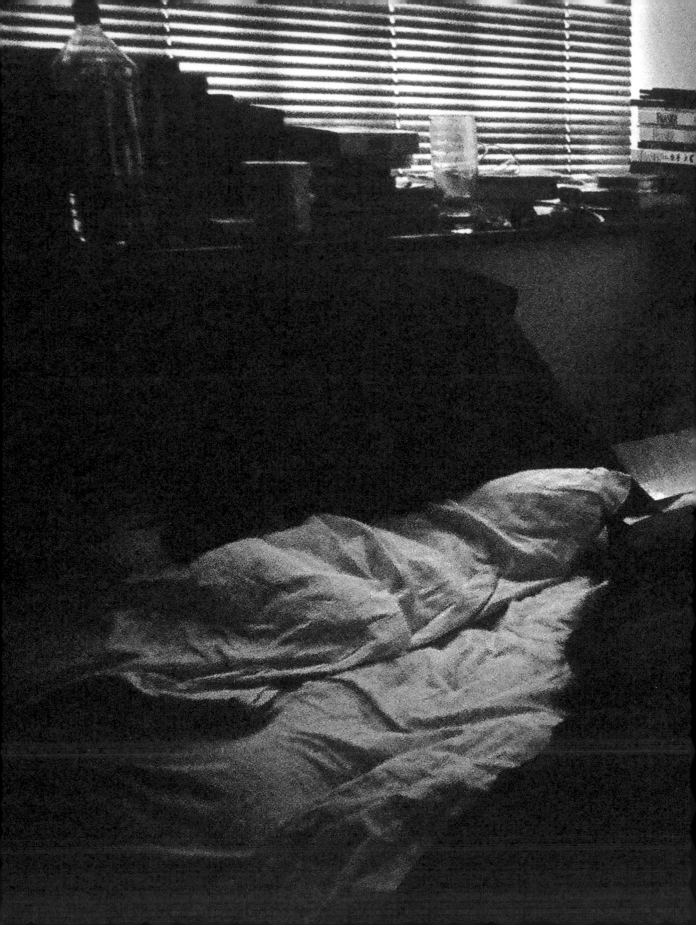

170

GARY CARD.

LONDON, ENGLAND

Gary Card is one of London's most talked-about young creative talents. A set designer, illustrator and prop maker, his work, which mixes bold and brightly coloured forms with darker and altogether more sinister elements, has won him clients including Comme Des Garçons, *The New York Times*, Topshop, Nike, Stella McCartney and British *Vogue*.

Card's home is an amalgamation of objects from previous creative jobs — chequerboard cardboard pillars housing cereal-box toys, hand-painted backdrops covering walls and framed shots of editorial commissions stacked on floors, surrounded by laundry bags. A perfectly honest and inspirational work and home space.

173.

174

177.

181.

OLEG DOU.

MOSCOW, RUSSIA

Oleg Dou's mother was a painter, his father was a dress designer, and he was brought up surrounded by artists. He experimented with computer design at an early age, later studied and practiced web design, then started taking photographs and creating unique, arresting computer-altered portraits. He was discovered in 2006 by the Russian Tea Room gallery in Paris, won a first prize at the International Photography Awards in 2008, and is now represented by galleries in France, Belgium, the Netherlands, Spain, Russia and the United States.

Dou's Moscow home, like his art, is starkly minimal with moments of comfort and safety. Scattered mannequin body parts and industrial tools contrast with soft woods and personal memoirs carefully placed. The shot I love the most is of the stunningly brutal view from his lounge out over a bleak, wet Moscow in late Autumn.

183.

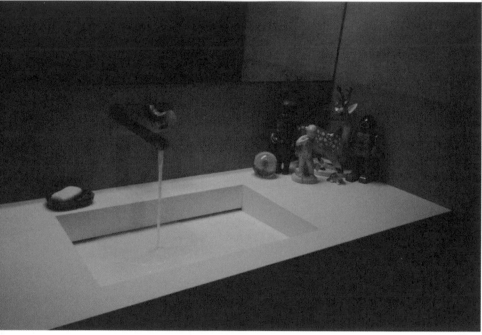

184

188

189.

MARC QUINN.

LONDON, ENGLAND

London-born artist Marc Quinn first gained notoriety as part of the YBAs (Young British Artists), a group which includes Damien Hirst and Tracey Emin. They began to exhibit together in the early 90s and were widely covered in the media for their shock tactics and use of throwaway materials. Quinn became known predominately for his sculpture pieces made out of materials ranging from blood, ice and faeces to bronze, marble and stone. His oeuvre is predominantly concerned with the mutability of the human body and the transience of life.

Quinn's west-London home is shared with his wife and two children, and constitutes the family living space as well as Quinn's studio, where he considerately covers his nude sculptures so the children don't see anything 'unsuitable'. The family also share their home with a beautiful pet owl — the only one in this book.

191.

192

197.

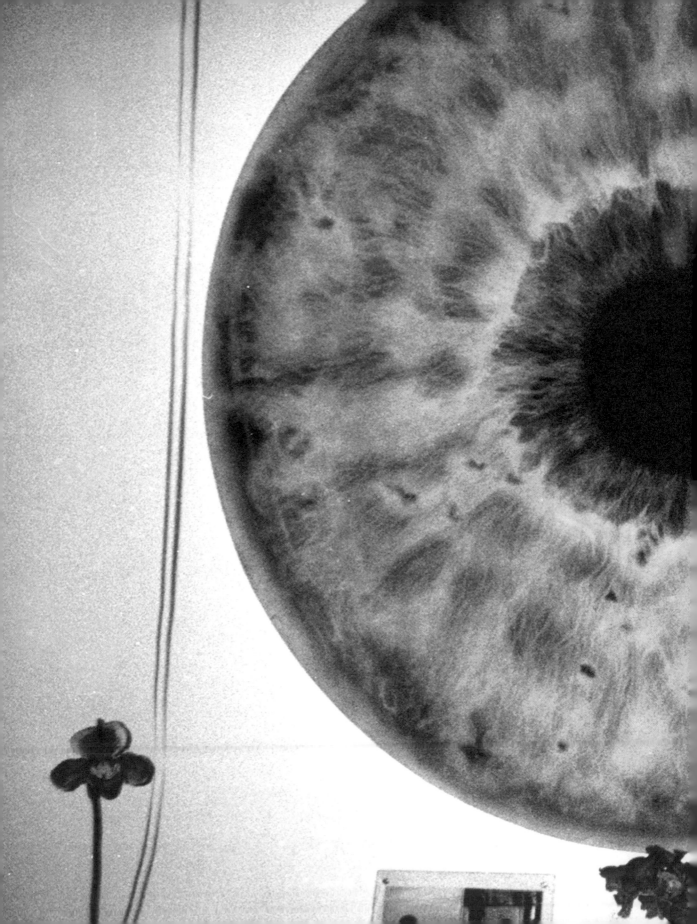

CONOR DONLON.

Conor Donlon first opened a small bookshop in 2005 at the back of the Herald St Gallery, below the studio of photographer Wolfgang Tillmans, whom Donlon assisted after graduating from Central St Martins. The success of that space led to him opening his independent shop, Donlon Books, in 2009 — a personally-curated boutique bookshop specialising in counterculture art, photography and music books.

A year after Donlon rented his shop, the flat above it became available. He lives there with his partner and it enables him to merge his home and work life. Indeed, the only exit from his flat is down the wooden spiral staircase that leads from his lounge straight to the shop floor. Both spaces have very similar dark wood styles, with mid-century and deco fittings, and the artworks move from shop to homespace effortlessly, and regularly — creating the ultimate in 'home office' interior style. It took two years for Conor Donlon to send back his disposable camera (after starting, not finishing and then losing four others!), but maybe this elusiveness has something to do with the success of his bookshop.

201.

202

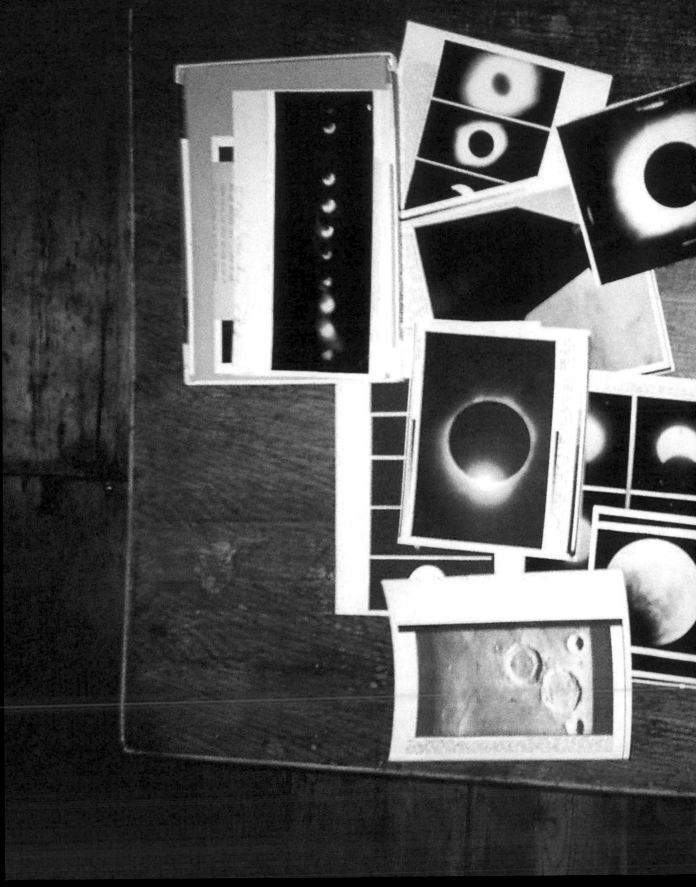

206

207.

TAVI GEVINSON.

CHICAGO, USA

Child fashion prodigy Tavi Gevinson first came into prominence in 2008, aged just eleven, through her popular blog Style Rookie. The rising journalistic star spent the next three years travelling the world (with her mum), reviewing international fashion weeks for the likes of *The New York Times*, *Harpers Bazaar* and Barneys, and appearing on the cover of *Pop* magazine herself, in a shoot by iconoclastic artist Damien Hirst. In 2011, she moved away from the fashion world, focusing instead on issues impacting teenage girls in her newly launched online magazine, *Rookie*. In both 2011 and 2012, Tavi appeared in the 'Forbes Under 30 in Media' list.

Now still only 16, she has quite the bright future ahead of her.

Tavi's home in Oak Park, Illinois (well, her parents' home, so predominately her bedroom), was photographed just as she was launching *Rookie* magazine and is filled with unusual inspirational references mixed with paraphernalia more typical to a teenage girl's bedroom. The best thing is her family fridge — an all-American dream.

217.

SIMON FOXTON.

LONDON, ENGLAND

Simon Foxton started his career at celebrated style magazine *i-D* in 1983, styled his first cover in 1987, and today, is its consultant fashion director. He has worked with some of the world's biggest fashion photographers and created culturally iconic images of London style since the mid-1980s. He has also contributed to international publications including *Fantastic Man*, *Arena Homme+* and *The Face* and consulted for brands like Stone Island and Nike. Foxton's work is held in collections at the Victoria and Albert Museum and the Tate Modern and the first ever exhibition devoted to a stylist's work, 'When you're a boy: Mens Fashion Styled by Simon Foxton', opened at London's Photographer's Gallery in 2009.

Foxton's home in south London could quite easily be a boutique hunting retreat in the rolling hills of Scotland or a ski lodge in the Canadian Rockies. This self-proclamied hoarder has filled his home with countless collections of objects, from walls of deer antlers to a dresser packed with milk glass toast racks. It's a strikingly busy space that you'll either love or loathe — but for me, it couldn't be a greater example of a home that is truly a labour of love.

223.

226

227.

228

MARTIN RAYMOND+ CHRIS SANDERSON.

LONDON, ENGLAND

Raymond and Sanderson are co-founders of The Future Laboratory, one of Europe's most influential trend forecasting consultancies, who can name clients such as American Express, Vodafone, Louis Vuitton, Burberry, Disney and Sony on their roster. Raymond is also a regular contributor on trends and business to *Wired* magazine, the BBC, Channel 4 and ITV, and is a Fellow of the Royal Society of Arts. Sanderson was previously Contributing Style Editor at *Esquire* magazine and UK communications director for Quicksilver and is now also a presenter on the Channel 4 technology show, *Home of the Future*. The couple bought their home in Whitechapel, east London, twenty years ago. Slowly but surely, they have turned the ramshackle Georgian townhouse into a striking display of tradition-meets-modernity.

The dark wood entrance hall opens onto a custom oak staircase complete with traditional 'trip steps' on all four floors; an incredible grass-walled 'entertaining space' filled with mid-century furniture leads upwards to Eastern-inpired sleeping quarters; and bookcases lining a corridor push open to reveal the pure white 'birds nest' lounge at the top of the house. The couple also have a much-loved art collection including pieces by Frank Stella and Rachel Whiteread, which is rotated round their living spaces.

233.

234

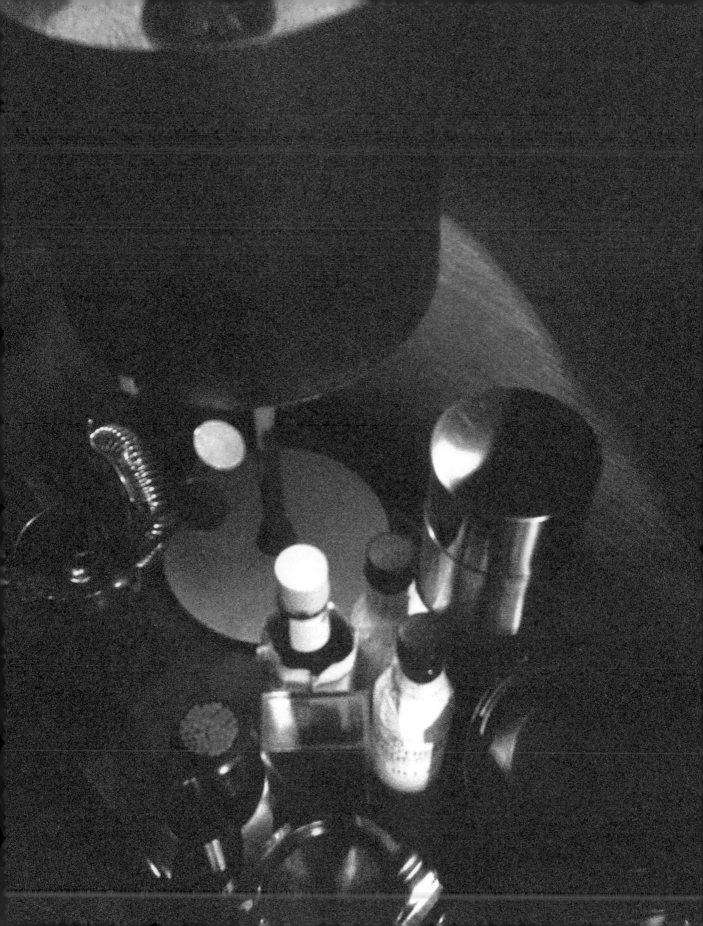

237.

NICOLA FORMICHETTI.

NEW YORK, USA

Nicola Formichetti's background is as diverse as his infamous work and style – the British-trained, Italian Japanese creative now resides in New York, while travelling between his clients in Tokyo, Paris and London, amongst other places. He cut his teeth as creative director at *Dazed and Confused* magazine, before becoming Lady Gaga's 'image maker'. Since then he has been artistic director at fashion house Mugler, fashion director at *Vogue Hommes Japan*, fashion director for Japanese high-street brand Uniqlo, and is now artistic director at Diesel. He is quite simply one of the most influential creative forces working in fashion today.

Nicola's interior style is, as you may expect, highly original and eclectic, from the 'jungle' you walk through to enter the apartment (including a five foot stuffed toy dinosaur) to the piles of Takashi Murakami signature flower cushions covering his Mexican-print-meets-modernist sofa. The apartment is filled with mementoes of his high-energy life and work style – from customised pieces made for Lady Gaga to his eponymous Nicopanda-graffitied Hermes 'Birkin' bags – and our favourite, custom-made monogrammed caps for his two Pomeranian puppies, Tank and Bambi (who also have their own Twitter accounts).

242

245.

249.

THANK YOU.

THE PEOPLE WHO INSPIRED THIS PROJECT

So, I suppose I start where the project began – a dusty, ramshackle Central Saint Martins' studio on Charing Cross Road in 2008, and four tutors who taught me that honesty and individuality is key – Judith Watt, Lee Widdows, Iain R Webb and Martin Andersen.

Next up, the people who have supported *Behind Closed Doors* since the beginning: thank you to *World of Interiors*' Creative Director Jessica Haynes for your constant belief in the project and Editor Rupert Thomas for writing the foreword. To the amazing team at *Garage Magazine*, who stepped in and helped me source a number of these incredible contributors – Dasha Zhukova, Becky Poostchi and the

amazing Holly Hay, thank you so so much. Also a big thanks to my mates and peers who have suffered the last few years of sourcing cameras, contacts and addresses, and giving me opinions on text, layouts, publishers, ideas and anything else I could possibly pick your brains about – notably, Ed Vince and Josh Gurrie.

And of course, a huge thank you to all those amazing contributors who have taken the time out of their lives to do this project: Vince Aletti, Gary Card, Conor Donlon, Oleg Dou, Nicola Formichetti, Simon Foxton, Tavi Gevinson, Terence Koh, Courtney Love, Aimee Mullins, Marc Quinn, Martin Raymond + Chris Sanderson, Jeremy Scott, Marvin Scott Jarrett, Christopher Simmonds, Lord Peregrine + Catherine St Germans, Martha Stewart, Matthew Stone, Kyle Stewart + Jo Sindle, Olivier Theyskens. And of course, my amazing

publisher, Kate Pollard, thank you so much for believing in this project; you will never know how much it means.

And finally, to my small but perfectly formed family, the ones who have always stood by the weird kid, stuck up for him, jibed him, kept his feet on the ground, and just been there, unconditionally – I love you all so much. Lastly, special mention to my dad, my eternal hero. xx

253.

THE AUTHOR.

A LITTLE ABOUT
ROB MEYERS

ob Meyers grew up in a small village in North Yorkshire to a mechanic father and interior design-based mother. At 18 he moved to London, where he still resides, to study communication design at seminal design school Central Saint Martins. Whilst studying he worked at style bibles *POP* and *Arena Homme+*, then did a stint in New York working for *Nylon* magazine, which is when the concept for *Behind Closed Doors* was born.

In late 2008 he set up design and creative direction agency RBPMstudio and has since worked for various brands and companies including Columbia Records, Burberry, Cos, Diesel, Luella, Jeremy Scott, ASOS, Nike, The Kings Cross development, *Nylon* and *World of Interiors* magazines, as well as some of the most exciting new designers on the London fashion scene.

In 2011 he took over the Creative Direction of magazine *Clash*, which went on to win 'Music Magazine of the Year' at the 2011/12 RODA Awards and is now Europe's highest selling independent music magazine.

www.RBPMstudio.co.uk
www.BehindClosedDoors.com
www.Rworks.com

255.

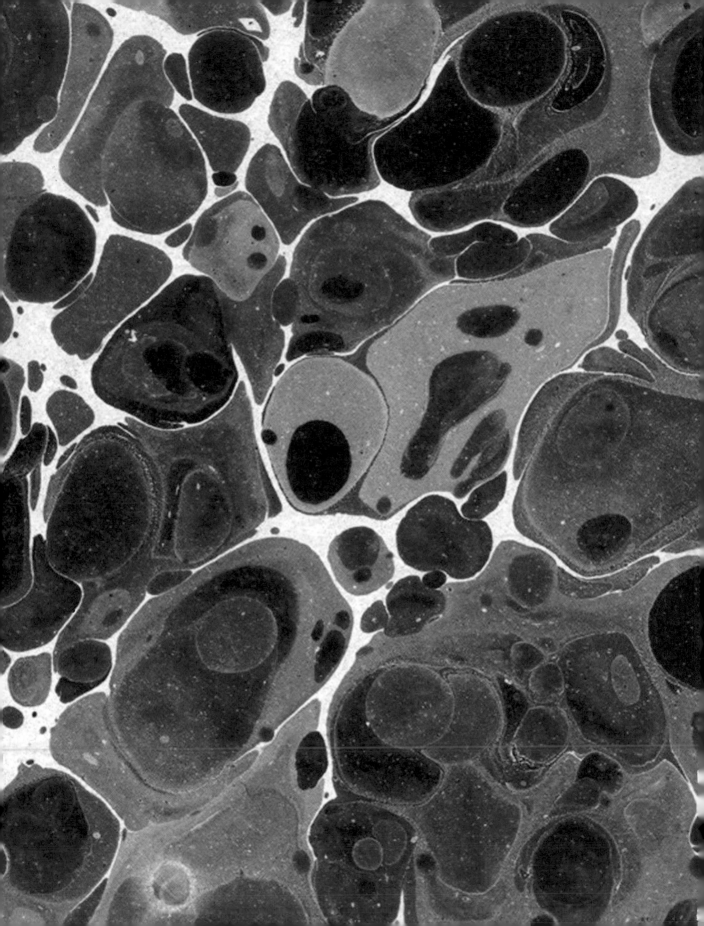